Philadelphia Watercolors

Philadelphia

Howard N. Watson

Introduction by John B. Kelly, Jr.

Barre Publishers
Barre, Massachusetts

Watercolors

© 1971 by Barre Publishing Co., Inc.

All rights reserved

Library of Congress Catalog Card Number 79–128386

Standard Book Number 8271–7022–X

Printed in the United States of America

T HE city of Philadelphia is like a member of my family. I may complain about it, or get mad at it, but I still love it and want the best for it.

Howard N. Watson is the only Philadelphia artist I know who has preserved the essence of this familial tenderness in his work. I am sure he returns as often as any painter of Philadelphia scenes to those areas of the city best known to those who see it in a cursory way, and are gone. But he feels strongly drawn to a side of Philadelphia loved only by those who have it in their bones—the neighborhoods, those ethnic villages that the developing city swallowed but did not digest; the red-brick tenements; the old burial grounds; the vastnesses of tarpaper rooftops; the pushcart markets; the Victorian rail stations; the jostling pavements of Race Street, buzzing in polyglot anticipation as the Chinese New Year's parade assembles around the corner.

Howard may soften the hard lines but the love sticks out all over. "My style kind of goes with the city," he told me recently. "It is easy for me to reflect, and feel, and enjoy the moods of Philadelphia. It is a great city to paint—almost Parisian."

Adopted sons often know the family best. Howard Watson came to Philadelphia as a young man from John O'Hara country, upstate Pottsville, where he was born more than forty years ago. The third and last son of an artist-photoengraver, Howard was torn between art and music, but he opted for the brush when his thirty-nine months in the Air Force were at an end in 1953. He studied painting at Temple University's Tyler School of Art, illustration at the Philadelphia College of Art. He and his wife, Julia—a gifted illustrator of children's books—live in a handsome old stone house in Germantown with their three children, and they live very graciously, I am happy to say, by their art alone.

For years I had known Howard Watson only through his watercolors, which I had admired at various exhibits and in the Sunday rotogravure pages of *The Philadelphia Inquirer*. When we finally met, the occasion was comparable to two strangers bumping into each other while paddling around in a vat of their favorite vintage wine—in our case, Port of Philadelphia. We both could have drowned smiling.

Philadelphia has been very good to me and it has been very good to my family, and I imagine Howard Watson would put it about the same way. I love this city very much. It has been in my marrow since I was a little boy in East Falls. I could no more divest myself of my Philadelphianess than I could zip out of my skin.

My father, in a sense, gave Philadelphia to me. I like to think of him as the greatest Philadelphian of them all, give or take a Benjamin Franklin or a Richardson Dilworth. He was a great athlete, politician, and builder (Philadelphia has an awful lot of bricks in it, and I can't look in any direction from my center city apartment today without seeing a building our company put up). He would have made a great mayor of Philadelphia had he run for office during a more enlightened period of Philadelphia politics. He didn't go beyond the eighth grade but he died a wealthy man and left more monuments to the living, quite aside from his buildings, than any man I can name. Just two of his projects — Kelly Pool, at Memorial Hall, and the Playhouse in the Park — have given joy to thousands of Philadelphians for many years.

My father infused in me a love of the city as painlessly as handing me an ice cream cone. He sent me to Penn Charter School, where the Quaker masters indoctrinated me well in the folklore of Philadelphia. When he was in politics and out visiting construction jobs he took me with him into the less attractive areas of town. I got to know and to appreciate the ethnic characteristics of the many Little Philadelphias. One place that left a lifelong imprint on me was the Italian market on South Ninth Street. I still marvel at the wonderful sights and smells, the vitality of the people and their openheartedness. There is a little restaurant on Ninth Street called the Villa DiRoma, where you are overdressed if you wear a clean T-shirt. Their mussels are magnificent. I feel as welcome there as I do at Old Original Bookbinders, that great Philadelphia eating institution where I often take out-of-town guests.

My father of course introduced me to Boathouse Row. I have spent so much of my life on the Schuylkill that I sometimes have the feeling it was I who modeled for Thomas Eakins when he painted his scullers. Today the river is murkier and the shoreline is very different in places, but Eakins would have no problem finding his way around. Philadelphia changes, but it takes its time about it, and maybe that's good.

My club for example, the Vesper Boat Club, dates from 1865. It is practically a newcomer on the scene. Nearly all of the nine existing clubs are well over a century old and the Schuylkill Navy is the oldest governing body in U. S. amateur sports. It is something to think about when the subject of cultural shock comes up. Cultural shock may be a useful phenomenon in bringing about needed social reforms more quickly. But none of us can exist for long in a world that does not stand still every so often, so that we may reflect, and cultivate a serenity of spirit, and let a sense of oneness with time and nature break over us. Only Philadelphia, of the major cities of this country, seems to me to have this elusive commodity to offer in accessible portions. Walk some afternoon behind the Museum of Art and toward the river, and wander under the classic porticoes of the Old Fairmount Waterworks. Within minutes you are carried in spirit to a state of timelessness, the pressures easing from the base of your neck.

I said at the beginning of this paean that I do get frustrated with my city-family once in a while, though never ceasing to love it. Certainly I would never trade off the charm of its antiquity or the life force of its cultural pockets for a mess of mendacious modern. I would move mountains, however, to liberate it from its conservatism. And moving mountains might be easier.

I am sentimental to the extent that I do not want to see City Hall, that most classic of extant Victorian masterpieces, razed, for it is a symbol of Philadelphia. I do want to exchange our eighteenth century image for at least a twentieth century one. Why, for example, should not the proposed northeast extension of the subway be conceived as an elevated monorail? Utilizing the center segment of the Roosevelt Boulevard, it could be built at much less than the cost of an underground line. It would cause tremendous excitement visually and it would symbolize a re-awakening of Philadelphia's dormant daring. This one concept could literally put the city on the move.

The 1976 Bicentennial Celebration may do for Philadelphia what Expo did for Montreal. It will make people think a little bigger. It will give them the idea that greater things can be done by and with and for the city. It will enlarge their outlook in many directions. It could even obliterate the slum scenes Howard puts on paper so eloquently.

Am I a dreamer? No. I am only a congenital Philadelphian — a Schuylkill basket case. At this moment I feel the need for a spiritual pick-me-up. A beaker of Howard Watson will save me a trip to the Old Fairmount Waterworks. Have one with me.

Jack Kelly

A note about Jack Kelly:

Jack Kelly is a widely known and handsome Philadelphian, the son of an equally well known Philadelphian of the same name. He won the single sculls championship at Henley in 1947 and 1949. He was a member of the U. S. Olympic Team in 1948, 1952, 1956, and 1960. He is a Philadelphia city councilman and president of the John B. Kelly Inc., a construction firm specializing in masonry. One of his three bright and beautiful sisters is Princess Grace of Monaco. He lives in the penthouse of a cylindrical high-rise overlooking Logan Circle and the Benjamin Franklin Parkway, and across the street from the three-story brick building which is his company's head-quarters. A pair of fine Howard Watson watercolors hangs among his old rowing prints.

Philadelphia Watercolors

Old Original Bookbinders at 2nd and Walnut Streets.

Logan Circle panorama, the most beautiful area in Philadelphia.

The magic of winter turns the green figures at Logan Circle into a frozen mountain.

A statue of George Washington guards the entrance to the Philadelphia Museum of Art.

Famous City Hall serves as a vantage point for William Penn.

Memorial Hall, the last building of the 1876 Centennial.

The Italian Market, where stall shopping is still very popular.

When summer comes the 'soul' people occupy the streets of North Philadelphia.

North Philadelphia's backyards tell the story of urban life.

Elfreth's Alley, only one block long, has changed little since Colonial days.

Looking down Broad Street towards City Hall.

Market Street, the heart of Philadelphia.

Philadelphia skyline at night.

Chinatown, where the community is preparing for Chinese New Year.

Old House in the Powelton section of West Philadelphia.

Market Street with its busy shoppers.

The Delaware River, with Ben Franklin Bridge crossing over to Camden, New Jersey.

Boat House Row located on the Schuylkill, in beautiful Fairmont Park.

The old Carpenter Station on the Chestnut Hill line.

The checker players sit in an old cemetery overlooking center city.

The West Philadelphia El, still the best transportation for the downtown shopper.

Independence Hall.

The old brick Head House and the once famous Second Street Market.

The Philadelphia Museum of Art stands on a hill hovering over the Schuylkill River.